DEDICATION

This book is dedicated to Almighty God, Agidi.Alex, Arun Chandran, my clients and students.

DISCLAIMER

The material in this book is not meant to be, and should not be interpreted or regarded as, financial advice. I am not an attorney, accountant, or financial counselor, and the material in this book is general and intended solely for educational reasons. The book is not a replacement for financial counsel from a professional who is familiar with the facts and circumstances of your specific situation.

We have done our best to guarantee that the material contained in this book is accurate and useful. Regardless of the contrary, nothing in this book should be interpreted as a recommendation that you should not speak with a financial professional to address your specific information. The writers and collaborators strongly advise you to seek professional guidance.

The Laws of Power in Financial Planning, Money Management, and Wealth Creation: A Handbook With a Practical Guide on Retirement Planning

JUSTIN S. REED

Copyright © 2022 Justin Reed

All rights reserved.

ISBN: 9798357415585

CONTENTS

DEDICATION	3
DISCLAIMER	4
CONTENTS	5
Introduction	7
LAW #1 AFFIRMATIONS	9
LAW #2 LAW OF ATTRACTION AND WEALTH	17
LAW #3 KEEPING YOUR ENERGY POSITIVE TO ATTRACT WEALTH	27
LAW #4 HAVE A CLEAR VISION	36
LAW #5 SET FINANCIAL GOALS	40
LAW #6 AVOID SHINY OBJECT SYNDROME	47
LAW #7 END FINANCIAL PRESSURE FROM PEERS/FAMILY	52
LAW #8 AVOID/ELIMINATE DEBTS	55
LAW #9 SAVE UP EMERGENCY FUNDS	61
LAW #10 CONTRIBUTE TO SEP-IRA	64
LAW #11 HAVE A GOOD HEALTH INSURANCE	66

LAW #12 HAVE AND FOLLOW A BUDGET 69

LAW #13 TRIM YOUR EXPENSES 73

LAW #14 IMPROVE YOUR KNOWLEDGE (Read Finance Books) 75

ABOUT THE AUTHOR 78

Introduction

Spending less than you earn is the first step towards generating wealth. Although it is easier said than done in today's world. The majority of individuals struggle with money management.

Financial buoyancy and stability comes with power, in economic terms "purchasing power". The power to get all you want when you want it and how you want to derive satisfaction or benefits from it, whereas this can only be possible if you are a good money manager. To be financially independent requires a high level of financial prudency. Those who win in life and business paid close attention to their finances.

Almost everything in the world has its own laws and principles. Law of attraction, law of gravity, law of thermodynamics, religious laws and doctrines, law of demand and supply and so on. People who don't apply the laws that are peculiar to their situation are doing themselves a great disservice. These laws are what guide and direct the affairs and activities of various successful and well to do people across different professions and engagements.

Money, which is an integral part of human socioeconomic existence, has principles guiding its acquisition and retention. Luckily for us, history has been so kind to offer us money management principles that have been proven and tested by financial experts, successful businessmen and world richest men. These principles should be employed by all who at some point in their life want to have power and control over their finances as well as those who want to live a life of financial independence now and for the rest of their lives.

A popular preacher once said "Financial rest does not come when you are a millionaire. It comes by being a good money manager. You must have a financial plan or else you are creating room for financial pain"

There are innumerable examples of millionaires who lost all of their money due to bad money management. Even the most successful individuals in any walks of life may go bankrupt if they lack sound financial judgment. Overspending, a lack of savings, and inadequate preparation for unforeseen circumstances like the covid-19 pandemic can all combine to create a perfect financial storm that wipes you out.

In this book, which contains over 2000 years old financial secrets, little known methods and principles. You will be exposed to LAWS that have made great men stay above all forms of financial crisis.

LAW #1 AFFIRMATIONS

Many years of financial stagnation may hurt one's prosperity mindset. It is not uncommon to see people struggling financially to keep asking themselves such niggling questions like:

- Do I deserve riches?
- Do I deserve all that I'm asking for?
- I don't even have what it takes to achieve all that!

Many individuals share this skepticism and think that our actions—or lack thereof—determine the level of riches we receive. You justify your current situation by looking at those doing well in life and business:

"She was wise enough to save a lot when she was young."

Since he had a high IQ, success was inevitable for him"

Guess what? Many individuals start saving early in life yet lose it all as a result of a catastrophe. Similar to this, there are a lot of individuals with brilliant ideas and high IQs. Many of these individuals are also homeless.

Imbibing good affirmation habits is based on the idea that you deserve to have all the money you want. Your foundation is your self-belief, the strong prosperity consciousness which you must first revamp to make room for plenty.

In other words, stop devoting time and effort to analyzing your personality and financial mistakes. This just serves to reinforce the notion that someone like you doesn't deserve money by keeping a continual, unrelenting emphasis on the bad decisions you believe you made.

In a nutshell. You deserve all you have right now.

And here is how you can verify that. Look at all the well-off folks around; those who don't have to worry about money and who can enjoy the present because they anticipate a happy future. Do you honestly, really think they never made a mistake with their finances?

They did, of course; everyone has. However, these are the people who didn't spend a lot of time beating themselves up. Instead, they offered themselves forgiveness, boosted their confidence, and eventually attained complete financial independence. They steadfastly resisted the idea that they weren't deserving of it.

The Key is in your head. You may use it to convince yourself that you are useless, which will make you feel that way. But, have this at the back of your mind; Worthlessness is not a magnet for wealth. Riches are rather drawn to assurance and the unwavering conviction that all you own is not only merited but also well-deserved.

Therefore, stop your train of thinking as soon as you find yourself being negative or realize that you have a pattern of criticizing yourself. Remind yourself that you only deserve the finest. Make use of that sharp intellect of yours, It will take practice since it might be difficult to overcome lifelong habits, so start small.

As soon as you notice that self criticism, alter it to "I deserve my prosperity." Just these four words should be used at the beginning. And now, you may be like, did he just say "my prosperity"?

Yes. Wealth already belongs to you. Simply having a strong conviction in it can help you find it. By claiming ownership, you are also putting yourself in a prosperous frame of mind.

Then, as you go about your day, say your affirmations aloud while feeling their reality. When you catch yourself thinking about your previous money situation, repeat your affirmations to yourself while paying close attention.

"I ought to have gotten a much less expensive automobile." Delete it. I MERIT MY PROSPERITY.

"Why did I purchase so many handbags? I don't need designer brands. Nope. I MERIT MY PROSPERITY.

If only I hadn't taken that vacation. Nonsense. I MERIT MY PROSPERITY.

I made a mistake by doing it alone. I ought to have stayed with a Monday through Friday job. Mistake again. I MERIT MY PROSPERITY.

"When I was younger, I indulged myself too much.

If I hadn't, I would currently have a lot more. How do we respond? In other words, I DESERVE MY WEALTH!

As often as you can, use affirmations. Say it every chance you get, including when you wake up and before you go to bed. Never explain, defend, or argue that you are deserving of prosperity. Simply comprehend what the universe is attempting to communicate. Your name is already inscribed on your fortune. All you have to do is be convinced and understand that you will get what is rightfully yours.

The simplest and most powerful strategy is to firmly declare that you deserve riches. Affirmations related to money replace negative thoughts with prosperous ones. They provide a screenplay to your mental faculty that attracts people, locations, and events into your life. Affirmations that inspire transformation are those that you create by seeing their reality in the here and now.

Here are five affirmations you may say aloud to banish negativity and firmly usher in riches.

"I Am Rich"

'Am'. Nothing that refers to the future. It's all

happening right now. This may sound absurdly straightforward, yet it is a strong affirmation that aids in diverting your attention from what you lack.

Say it both before you go to sleep at night and when you get up in the morning. When you consider that credit card statement, say it. Say it frequently and let it sink in. Wealthy people don't go about with hunched shoulders and drooping heads. Say that with a smile on your face and the conviction that you are fortunate.

"I'm Set On Accepting Financial Freedom"

Freedom, according to Kris Kristofferson, "is simply another term for nothing left to lose." You are aware that this isn't always the case. However, being able to realize all of your aspirations is freedom. You may have fantasized about enjoying a glass of wine while looking out at the Eiffel Tower. The list goes on. Perhaps you want to purchase a house in the country, someplace you could ride a horse peacefully. Reiterate your readiness for financial independence in your affirmations. Recognize that your dreams will come true, and be ready to accept them.

"All Bills Are Paid"

As the debts increase, so does your stress. Remind yourself that "Every bill is paid". Make careful to avoid using "will be paid". The purpose is to reassure oneself that your bills have already been paid. Feel the joy and pleasure of covering all your monthly bills and yet having money to spare. Keep that happiness and sense of security alive.

"I Effortlessly Receive Wealth, and I Accept It"

You can utilize this one every day, especially when you find yourself pondering how you'll manage to receive what you're requesting. We have been taught that to become very wealthy, a strategy must be in place. Planning is a wonderful thing, but it's not always successful. Just speak with those who have been impacted by Ponzi scams or the subprime mortgage crisis. Allow money to flow to you easily. Avoid attempting to predict how it will occur. Simply have faith that it will and always be prepared to receive it.

"I Can Live With Great Wealth"

Sometimes, the brain sneers uncontrollably at the notion of a common person just obtaining an enormous fortune. This is probably due to the idea that we don't deserve anything if we don't go through hardship and make sacrifices for it. Consequently, you feel a bit bad about having as much money as you desire. Put an immediate stop to that emotion.

There is enough money to go around, and

everyone ought to have as much as they desire. There's no need to feel bad. Instead, concentrate on enjoying your money.

Finally, everyone is familiar with the story of Steve Jobs quitting college due to financial difficulties. But did he ever imagine that he would live in poverty forever? Not at all. He attended courses after school quietly, and there was a calligraphy course among them. He started Apple six months later, which created the first computer with attractive, creative font styles. Apple stood out from the start because of its creativity. What follows is history. Hold on to your conviction that you can attract prosperity. Utilize the affirmations for assistance. and see how your life's journey plays out.

LAW #2 LAW OF ATTRACTION AND WEALTH

The universe is generous. You can always ask for something and get it. That's actually how easy it is. The universe, like everything else, is subject to rules. Additionally, the law of attraction thrives on a foundation of positiveness. And you may ask, how can you stay positive? After all, you've been through and still going through. How will that be possible when the news and social media are constantly flooding us with tragic tales of conflict, brutality, and murder of all kinds? How can you find joy when your account is almost empty and your rent is due? Even people with the brightest personalities find it difficult.

Sometimes, life just happens. You might be financially squeezed, anxious, and worn out if you become sick, or get divorced, among many other things. It's possible that none of the aforementioned things happen and that you just made one or more poor decisions. Nevertheless, stop criticizing yourself right this second. Do you know who else has made poor decisions? All those who haven't admitted to it. There is not a single one of us who has never made a financial mistake. But they go on with confidence rather than allowing their errors to intimidate them.

But after disaster or errors, how can you regain your composure and positivity? Everyone has their technique, but creating a vision board is a fast and easy solution. A vision board is exactly what it sounds like: a large surface on which you may cut and paste all of your heart's desires in their order of importance. The law of attraction stresses the importance of consciously imagining your fortune.

Additionally, having a vision board is beneficial since you can quickly glance at it for confirmation rather than taking a deep breath, shutting your eyes, and daydreaming about a lavish beach vacation. The five steps highlighted below will help you make a successful vision board.

Build Two Vision Board: The first vision board you create will serve as a template for the second. The positive aspects of your history will be represented on your first vision board. Be quite creative with this. Give your credentials, if you have any, a spot on the board if you are proud of them. Include photographs of your kids if you have any. Anyone raising children in this difficult environment is performing an incredible feat. Maybe your dog was sick, and you took care of her until she was well again. Post a picture of her on the wall. Look for "thank you" messages, referral letters, successfully finished projects, cards from your children, or anything else that demonstrates your power and tenacity. You know you do, after all.

Make A Space: Make room for both of your boards before moving on to the second one. You may wish to hang them close to your workstation if you work from home. If you're a housewife, attach them to the kitchen cabinet doors (a refrigerator door may be too small). How about the hot desk at your job at an office? It's no issue. Get two thin scrapbooks and take them with you everywhere you go. Take every opportunity to sneak a glance.

Gather Information: The diagram you have available will undoubtedly affect what you write on the board, even though this may seem like a no-brainer. Your vision board could be depressing if all you have are outdated news magazines. Make sure you get a range of magazines as they are a great source. Inquire about the availability of your pals. You may also ask for magazines in the waiting areas of hair salons, nail salons, and physicians' offices. Google is undoubtedly another option. Look for wide classifications. If you wish to travel, for instance, search for "luxury trip". Browse whenever you like, print, and save.

Describe Your Vision: The exciting part comes next. But hold on a second. Look at the first board you have. Look at you, you are amazing. Allow yourself a moment to enjoy it and feel admirable. Proceed to board 2 now. How do you see things? What do you envision for the future? Utilize the first board's quality to fuel and energize the one you're working on right now. Do you want to travel in luxury at all times? Any airline should have a photo of a first-class cabin. Include any hotel rooms you'd want to stay in. Decide on a landscape. Do you like the city, the desert, the mountains, the beach, or the forest? You are not obligated to choose, but you may. Put each of them on the board. Duplicate your most recent credit card statement and white out the amount if your biggest concern is credit card debt. To make it seem as if you owe nothing, now enter $0.00. Checks are the last component that needs to be on your board. There are a ton of examples available online that you can simply print off if you'd prefer not to use one of your own. Fill up the recipient field with your name, followed by the desired amount. Because uncertainty often enters at this point, the focus is placed on what you "want." Once you've completed that, provide the date on which you anticipate receiving this money. Insert the check into the board. And lastly;

Carefully Handle (And Fun): Enjoy yourself while creating the board. Feel free to make the images more engaging as this should be a fun practice. Use doodling, gold star stickers, or favorite quotes—anything that makes you feel warm and cheerful. Each image you post on the board deserves respect. Handle this image of your life carefully since it represents a life that is simply waiting for you. Once your boards are finished, carefully examine them. The first one demonstrates your uniqueness and serves as more evidence that you are deserving of every item on your second board. As frequently as you can, scan the boards. Take solace and security from them. Having an affirmation on hand could even be helpful. The phrase "This is my life and I embrace it" is one proposal. Modify as required if it doesn't suit you. Say that again and mean it. Anyone who is acquainted with the law of attraction will recognize how straightforward the idea is. What you genuinely desire will materialize if you only imagine it in your head, and the universe will make every effort to do it.

Sounds straightforward, right?

Yes. Though it seems easy in principle, it is challenging to put this concept into practice. We, humans, emotional beings, and the ups and downs of life have an impact on our emotions, thoughts, and behavior. But the law of attraction calls for constant optimism and trust in the face of impossibility. It needs you to be the bright spot that cuts through the gloomy mist of doubt and pessimism. It will take a lot of work and constant concentration to get to this point. You'll have to put in a lot of effort. This is not a simple task.

We're going to go into depth about each point rather than providing you two lists of dos and don'ts since, most of the time, a don't result from not doing what you're meant to. Even though the law of attraction has helped millions of individuals, they still make up a small percentage. The majority of individuals who attempt it will fail badly and fail to attract anything, much less fortunate. Let's examine the cause of this.

Be Specific;

You must first know EXACTLY what you desire to attract it into your life. There are no gray areas in the universe. You must be precise. If you wish to materialize an automobile, you must know its model, color, and whether it will be brand-new or used. Yes, even if it's only for visualization, you need that amount of information. Knowing exactly what you want is half the battle won. Be specific. Don't be ambiguous.

Emotions are everything;

Once you've decided what you want, you HAVE to behave as if you already have it. Feel the happiness and thrill of achieving or receiving what you had imagined. Emotion is fundamental. Emotion is the key that opens the door to anything your heart wishes in terms of the law of attraction. So many folks get off to a good start and feel enthusiastic. However, individuals lose their joy and optimism when their desired outcome takes longer than expected. They wind up acting robotically and without "heart." Therefore, nothing ever materializes. Your whole body must be filled with unshakeable faith. When practicing visualization, keep your emotions and trust under check. Don't follow a boring routine.

Action is The Foundational Key To Success;

This is the section that was left out of the film "The Secret." action+attract =attraction. Too many individuals think that visualizing alone can accomplish their goals. Nothing is more false than this. "God provides every bird its food, but He does not toss it into its nest," American author J.G. Holland famously stated. You can still comprehend the quote's main point even if you don't consider yourself religious. You must do every effort to realize your ambitions. Think positively, have faith, and act.

When you exert every effort to achieve your goals, the universe will open doors and provide you with possibilities you never dreamed possible. Although it may appear accidental, the law of attraction is rewarding you for your efforts. Do be an action taker. Don't just sit around.

Attitude of Gratitude;

You should always be thankful for what you have, no matter how difficult it may be. You may not enjoy the position you're in, but endeavor to be appreciative of the benefits that you do have. You would see that you have many things to be thankful for if you took the time to look. your ability to see, your health, having a place to live, etc. We often feel unhappy because we think we haven't received what we deserve. Or we see others who seem to be doing better than us, and we are envious of them and want what they have. You must practice gratitude to use the law of attraction. Then it will provide you with more rewards. That is just how things are. Your predicament will only grow worse the more you moan and whine about it. With a negative outlook, you cannot attract good things. Do exercise patience and gratitude. DO NOT whine or despise your lot in life.

Repetition;

Constant repetition carries conviction, as the author Robert Collier famously put it. You must imagine at least once or twice a day in order to practice the law of attraction. This scenario is challenging. You must envision with faith as often as you can. But you shouldn't, because of doubt, do it repeatedly. There is a difference in this. It will be far more advantageous to envision once a day with trust and conviction than to do it twenty times out of frustration at not yet having what you desire. The universe cannot be hurried. Be constant, yet refrain from mindless repetition.

In conclusion, the law of attraction is true, but you

must learn to manage your thoughts and exercise self-discipline. You can master the law and bring miracles into your life. But, first you must master yourself. Everything begins with you. That's the real secret.

LAW #3 KEEPING YOUR ENERGY POSITIVE TO ATTRACT WEALTH

Have you ever observed that excellent individuals seem to draw around you when you're feeling fantastic on the inside and out? Consider a scenario in which you had a great day at work, a restful night of sleep, and a party to attend that evening. You're likely to have a good experience that you'll remember. There is no chance behind this. You would have been radiating a happy, upbeat, and motivating aura that would have drawn the appropriate individuals to you. You would have had fascinating discussions and possibly come away with one or two new friends. We've all been in situations like this. The secret behind this is that we are all capable of sensing energy.

Now, in the same line, would you agree that you may use your energy to attract riches and other positive things if you can draw intriguing, genuine individuals to you in only a few hours?. I guaranteeess your answer is Yes!.

According to science, Two major things make up the world (matter and energy) while energy is said to cover a huge 70%. So it's okay to say energy makes up everything in the world, including riches. Your manager can request that you put in more hours if your business is experiencing an extremely busy moment. Work must be brought home, even on weekends. Your employer arranges a dinner as a token of gratitude after the busy season. There, she announces that your bonus will increase by 30% as a result of all your hard work in making your firm successful.

Now, try to picture that scenario.

Imagine attending the meal right now. Does your list of possible purchases come to mind as soon as your employer mentions the bonus increase? Or is your first response to bask in the sunshine of gratitude?

The latter is most likely the case since money carries its vitality. You put in a lot of effort, sacrificed a lot of your free time, and most likely missed many important events. You were acknowledged and praised after all that. You're satisfied with it and would probably do it again. Why?, Because you gave your energy in return for recognition of your efforts and a respectable financial recompense.

Let's do a little experiment now. Recall the time when you were working hard, feeling worn out, and perhaps feeling a little disappointed. You've reached the end of this rough stretch. Your supervisor then orders you all to return to your regular job duties without so much as a "thank you."

What emotions come to mind first?

You would likely feel frustrated, resentful, and most of all, exhausted. Why?, Because there was no energy transfer. Contrary to the bonus scenario, it was taken from you and not returned. Money has many uses than merely the ability to be spent on items. Its energy affects how you feel. More significantly, the amount of money you draw to yourself is directly related to your energy. This is the reason why proponents of the law of attraction stress the importance of maintaining a good attitude. Recall the party and how your enthusiasm drew genuine, thoughtful individuals to you. With money, you may achieve the same results. But, you wonder, how? "I have a job I despise and am deeply in debt." Anyone in such a circumstance would expect to feel as if they had spent the night carrying a load of boulders. Maintaining a cheerful outlook indeed requires practice. The good news is that as you read this piece, you may begin right now.

Debt;

Debt is a cruel master who makes you feel sick to your stomach whenever you think about it. It puts you down, assigns blame, and takes your sleep stealthily like a robber in the night. The majority of us fall into that trap. We concentrate on the debt and as we do, we imbue it with more and more power. By doing this and concentrating on our deficiencies, we draw scarcity to ourselves. How can you transform this into a positive? Start by letting debt go of its place as the main focus of your day and your extended, restless evenings. Flip it as soon as you notice yourself thinking about all the money that is in the negative. Look at the same quantity in black in your imagination. That is the amount of money in your bank account, tell yourself. Sense it. Act it. Own it. By doing this, you will start to attract methods to pay off the awful "D" word in addition to repelling scarcity. And keep a close eye on your finances because it won't end there!

Embarrassing Jobs;

Let's be honest. Nobody's notion of a nice existence is being locked in a job they despise, surrounded by treacherous coworkers, and having a violent boss. But due to its usefulness, we continue with it. Anything else would be too dangerous. mostly because we must eat. And it is awful every day.

Let's revisit the guests who were drawn to your business at that gathering. The same idea also applies to the work you do. Start by concentrating on one good item you are doing at work. It may be that wonderful coffee shop just around the corner from the workplace. Because you work there, you get to enjoy that wonderful coffee. Enjoy your beverage. savor the scent. Look forward to that cup of coffee every day. What relevance does any of this have? A good question. The coffee (or muffin, deli sandwich, or hot dog) gives you a quick method to change your outlook on your work. Find the one thing that makes your day a little bit happier. You'll feel happier the more focus you put on it. You'll be more confident in attracting riches and happiness if you feel more upbeat. A boss who values you and offers you a fair increase may take the place of a bully. This fosters a positive working culture that results in contented coworkers. Of course, fulfillment may not occur as the exact illustration given above. Your optimism and self-assurance will draw in a huge variety of wonderful things that I am unable to name. You just need to begin right now. But, what if you are unemployed right now;

Unemployment;

Unemployment may completely catch you off guard or it may have been going on for some time. It is natural to also have a sense of uneasiness while you are between jobs, but it may be difficult to get over. The jobless often battle to remain optimistic and strong for their families and loved ones, but who supports them?. It may be challenging to confess anxiety and worry, especially for guys. However, it is harder and harder to remain positive as time goes on and chances of finding work grow more remote. At first, being unemployed could have looked like a relaxing break. But soon, a sense of isolation and hopelessness sets in, and everything appears gloomy. Depression, social isolation, weight gain, and bad behaviors may all develop into routines. However, there are methods to avoid these risks and make an effort to go around them. You may maintain the best health for your mind by following these suggestions.

Be realistic: Verify your emotions. Your income has

diminished, the future is unclear, and you may not feel like you have a purpose in life. Your world has not, however, ended. Not everything about who you are as a person is reflected in your job. Recognize that you are greater than your circumstance and be realistic about the timetable for finding another job.

Make objectives: Consider researching one new employment lead every day. You may plan on making five calls each day. Maybe you'll try to connect with one new individual each week. Keep to that timetable in any way you feel is sensible and beneficial for your circumstances.

Always keep your eyes on the future: Every day, assess your circumstances. Make a list of everything you've done so far and consider what has and hasn't worked. Make sure you're keeping an eye out for new employment openings that might act as a short-term safety net. You could even decide to completely change your job path and pursue a new one that is more in line with your true preferences. The secret is to have a positive outlook on the future and make sure you have a backup plan at all times. You are in a fantastic position to emerge from this difficult adjustment stronger than you were before as long as you are keeping active, maintaining structure, and depending on a solid support system.

Spend time with other people: When jobless, it may

be quite simple to isolate oneself, which is a bad mistake. You can feel too embarrassed to get out with your pals and believe that you don't even deserve to be sociable. However, the reality is that you need the encouragement of dependable friends and family to stay motivated. Although we are excellent at motivating ourselves, it is risky to depend only on our sense of worth. Instead of isolating yourself, surround yourself with positive individuals who will motivate and inspire you. When it comes to finding a new job, a friend may be a huge assistance.

Keep your life organized: If you don't have a job, you can tend to remain in bed all day, go out late at night, and sleep too little or too much while staying in bed all day. This is because if we begin to wander every day or adapt to an unhealthy or foreign lifestyle, we risk losing our sense of direction and purpose. Although getting to sleep till noon may seem wonderful at the time, you'll eventually regret it or feel as if your week was squandered. You'll be more goal-oriented and prepared to rejoin the workforce if you maintain a routine.

Utilize free resources: You will feel the tension and worry in varying degrees when jobless, therefore it's important for you to hunt for answers. Consider visiting the library to seek publications on managing stress and how to do it successfully. There are a ton of incredible low-cost and free tools available to assist with job searching as well as stress management. Also, Check out the "takechargeamerica.org" website to see if you can find organizations that provide consumer help and stepping stones for the jobless if you're looking for work or finding it difficult to pay your bills each month.

LAW #4 HAVE A CLEAR VISION

In the words of the Canadian educator Lawrence J. Peters "if you don't know where you are going, you will probably end up somewhere else." To some people, It may seem like a pointless, unrealistic waste of time to develop a financial vision, but this is not the case. Developing a compelling financial vision is one of the most powerful ways to live the life of your dreams. Perhaps the best way to see the idea of a vision is as a compass to assist you in choosing the best course of action and making decisions that will help you move toward your best life. Your financial vision should be able to motivate you to pursue financial independence. Of course, as you become older and earn more money, your perspective on money will change.

Also, Your financial goals are all part of your financial vision. What picture comes to mind when you think of retiring? Here is one of my tips for making a smooth transition. Have a unique vision for this next stage of your life. Why? Having a clear understanding of your goal is the cornerstone of a shift that goes well. That is what separates a desire from a goal. Additionally, you should be clear on the principles that will direct your life going forward since doing so will enable you to spend more time on the aspects of your life that are important to you. Many self-help professionals and authors agree that having a goal in mind increases your chances of success considerably above what you may otherwise accomplish in the absence of a clear vision. Having a long-term perspective on your finances not only guarantees your future but also eliminates tension and fear from your present. For example;

Vision: I want to retire early.
Clarity of purpose: I want to retire at 45 years old.

Remember that there is no one "correct way" that is just waiting to be discovered for you. There are a ton of options from which to pick. Therefore, clarity is crucial. Consider the example above! If you want to retire at age 45, you'll need to start saving regularly and investing early to keep up with inflation and lifestyle changes. Clarity cannot be attained by just accepting each day as it comes. You can see where you're going with the aid of your vision. This is what's referred to as clarity my friend, and you need it. Indecision, uncertainty, and hesitancy, which are all preventing you from achieving your objectives, are the opposite of clarity. Those problems are a result of not having a specific goal in mind. Before you start, you need to know where you're going. Otherwise, you'll spend time trying to figure out where you are and feeling a little panicky because you're lost (which you are since you didn't know where you were going in the first place). You may overcome obstacles by staying focused on your vision.

    I won't lie; reaching your objectives will need a lot of effort. There will be difficulties and days when you won't feel it at all. Even though you'll be worn out and experience disappointments, your inspiration to keep going on comes from seeing how things will be after all of your hard efforts. The sad truth is that if you don't create your vision, you'll let other people and external factors decide how your life will turn out. A clear and well-defined vision won't appear overnight; it takes time and thought to picture your future and decide on your plan of action. For the practical implementation of your idea, you must cultivate perspective and vision as well as use logic and preparation. Your highest desires are the seeds from which your best vision will grow. Your values and ideals will be reflected in it, and it will inspire vigor and passion to support your resolve to explore your life's potential. Find and read about people whose lives you admire. Look into how they got where they are and why they do what they do. Perhaps even see if you could meet with them in person. Reading about those who've survived financial crises is even better as you can learn a lot from them. Think about how you want your life to be. Envision an end goal. What do you want the pattern of your life to be? What kind of a guy would you want to be? What kind of family do you want to have? What kind of profession are you interested in? Visualize it and describe it in great detail. Construct a mission statement and a set of objectives. Consider a single statement that sums up your vision. Put it in writing and in a visible location. Then, list three to five actions that you will do over the next several months to get closer to realizing your vision. Create new ones after you've completed the previous ones and so on.

LAW #5 SET FINANCIAL GOALS

Now that you can see your future, you must create a strategy to assist you in achieving your objectives. "If you want to be happy, set a goal that commands your thoughts, liberates your energy, and inspires your hopes." Andrew Carnegie.

Setting financial objectives for the short, medium, and long term is a crucial first step toward achieving financial freedom. Without a clear goal in mind, you run the risk of going overboard with your spending. Then, when you need money for unforeseen expenses, not to mention when you want to retire, you won't have enough. You can find yourself mired in a cycle of credit card debt and feel as if you never have enough money to be adequately insured, making you more exposed than you need to be to tackle some of life's biggest challenges. As the globe discovered during the covid19 pandemic and unanticipated economic recessions, even the most careful individual cannot adequately prepare for every disaster. By planning, you have the opportunity to consider potential outcomes and make every effort to be ready for them. This has to be a continuous process so that you can adapt your life and ambitions to the changes that are unavoidably going to occur. Take advantage of the chance to create objectives if you haven't done so before so that you may establish or maintain a solid financial foundation. You may consider your financial goals, but achieving that idealized vision of personal finance requires a detailed strategy that you can implement. Setting goals may help you break down a huge goal into manageable stages, enabling you to feel more accomplished as you approach the goal. This encouraging feedback might give you some momentum and encourage you to keep going, especially for any potentially challenging phases that may be ahead. Unfortunately, most individuals lack the dedication, persistence, and tenacity necessary to remain on course until they achieve their goals. This is why Financial experts recommend setting SMART GOALS.

What are SMART GOALS?

The acronym SMART is used to describe the following 5 criteria that a goal ought to have:

- S— Specific
- M–Measurable
- A— Achievable
- R— Relevant
- T— Time-bound

Let's examine the meanings of these terms now.

- Specific: The first thing to keep in mind while creating a SMART objective is that it has to be specific. For instance, if you earn a considerable good amount of money but often go cashless and want to change that, you may set the following as your goal: "I want to save some money this month! " is a noble but unwise objective. It needs to be precise. How much money are you aiming to save? Ten thousand? Five thousand? A specific objective might be, "I want to save Three thousand dollars this month." Excellent, but our work is not yet done.

- Measurable: What is measured gets done when it comes to money. You may check your account balance often to make sure that your goal of saving 10% of your monthly income is being met. Setting such objectives is a method to hold yourself responsible for your progress toward achieving financial stability. Is there a means to track your progress in the aforementioned example? Yes, there is. To determine how much you have saved so far, you may get a financial planner or use a calendar and tick each date as you save. But ensure you stick to a specific amount like $50, $100, or $500 on each date. There has to be a method to gauge your growth. How will you gauge your success in reaching your savings goals? How can you possibly know? A quantifiable objective might be helpful. Setting a goal to save $500 every 2 days if you presently save $200 will be quantifiable, but you'll obviously need to be more financially viable to achieve it. Therefore, make sure you can track your improvement at all times.

- Achievable: Given how often big thinking and ambitious dreams are discussed, this is a complicated issue. It's a wonderful idea to strive to be financially free, but you also need to be reasonable. Your objective of saving $100k in six months is NOT attainable if you earn below $20k monthly. It could seem inspiring and have a lot of "oomph! " aspect to it, but if you don't do it in phases, you'll never pull it off. The first step is to get rid of all of your unnecessary expenses. After doing that, you may go to the next stage and so on. Set manageable objectives that won't overwhelm you in the near future. like, saving $50k in 6 months if you earn $20k or less monthly.
- Relevance: You don't have to do anything just

because you can. You must honestly consider if your objective is something you desire. Goal-setting is all too often motivated just by envy of others' possessions. Your objective can be to become a millionaire, for instance if you're motivated by the lifestyle photographs that some folks post on social media regularly. Is that what you desire, though?. Most folks would be more than content to earn $50,000 a year more than they do now. They may not be able to make the sacrifices necessary to achieve a million dollars, and why should they when they'll be content with earning $150,000 annually? Therefore, consider what you want and if your objective is in line with your ideals and something essential to you.

• Time-bound: Robert Herjavec, a Canadian businessman, famously said: "A goal without a deadline is simply a dream." This is true. A deadline is necessary for a set objective to give your project momentum. Again, we need to remain grounded in reality. Rome wasn't constructed overnight, but every hour, bricks were being laid. As an example, if you want to have $50k savings at the end of a year. This could mean you need to save $1k weekly or $4,200 every month. That indicates that it will take you 50 or 52 weeks to save that amount. This duration is reasonable. Especially, if you have a lot of bills to pay from your monthly earnings. It takes longer than normal. What if you aimed to save all fifty thousand dollars in just six months? When you earn below $10k monthly. This duration is utterly unlikely. No matter how much you cut down expenses, it is quite unlikely that you will succeed in this aim, and even if you do, it won't be healthy or sustainable. Setting a more acceptable timeframe would be preferable. Don't get upset or worry if you don't reach your objective by the deadline. Such could happen. Worthwhile projects often take longer than anticipated. Depending on the objective, extend the deadline by one or more months while continuing to make progress without flagging. This is how you reach your objectives.

Now that you are aware of the SMART method of goal-setting, assess your present financial goals to determine whether they meet these requirements. Once you've established your SMART goals, keep them in front of you every day (and write them down every day) to internalize them in your memory and ensure that you work consistently in line with them until you reach your goals. Keep in mind that life occurs while you consider your financial objectives. Unexpected job loss, a huge expenditure for medical care, or any other significant event might throw your original plan of action off course. This might include changing your objectives or pausing your plans for a time until you can resume them. Additionally, it could result in completely different objectives and priorities.

Whatever happens, do the needful by ensuring you have a financial goal to be met when you can.

LAW #6 AVOID SHINY OBJECT SYNDROME

Massive distraction results from pursuing new opportunities constantly and accepting too many assignments without considering how they relate to your goals.

Shiny object syndrome may be the cause of your persistent interest in trends and pursuit of new endeavors.

Shiny object syndrome refers to the propensity to continuously seek out new possibilities, trends, and ideas without properly weighing their merits.

Shiny object syndrome results in loss of focus, distraction and other negative effects.

Additionally, going after new aims rather than concentrating on your goals will cause you to lose crucial time. Basically, shiny object syndrome is when a person gives something fresh and trending their undivided attention and most people do this at the expense of their ongoing tasks.

Shiny objects syndrome also known as SOS could destroy your financial goals. It doesn't matter if you've a beautiful financial plan written down and well laid out. You will have financial problems if you suffer from SOS. Not being able to follow through on a business dealings or contracts before jumping on another might affect how much you make in that financial cycle and this will affect your ability to save up for emergency and other financial goals. If you constantly jump on trends like the urge to get some new popular items such as the latest Apple products or Sneakers might mean you are suffering from shiny objects syndrome. This would negatively affect your financial plans. Below are 2 major methods to curb the negative influence of shiny objects syndrome.

The first one is to analyse the positive side of the shiny object. Even though I advise against grabbing the next shiny thing that crosses your path, there are situations when its potential influence surpasses the cost implications. New products are continuously being developed and released onto the market, and some of them may be just what you or your business needs to boost productivity or financial wellbeing. However, you should consider how the product or service may affect your long term financial goals or business. Moreover, maintain objectivity. By doing this, you can make better decisions and determine whether the product or service will benefit you or your financial plans.

Let's now discuss "lifestyle creep."

Lifestyle creep is a prevalent phenomenon whereby people spend more money as their income increases and come to accept higher standards of luxury and comfort as the new normal. Lifestyle creep generally happens after someone receives a pay increase, accepts a new position with a greater salary, or eliminates debt. For instance, when your salary rises, you start driving a fancier automobile, eating at pricier restaurants, and so on. Your bills will rise along with your expenses , and because you are still not saving much money, you'll discover that your financial condition doesn't truly get better. Even if you're earning more, you can still be in debt and live paycheck to paycheck.

Is this new expenditure truly necessary?

No, but you want it because everyone else has it and are raving about it. Now that gives you the fear of missing out. Do you really want your expenses to go up because of this?. It gets very expensive when lifestyle creep and shiny item syndrome are combined. Avoid unnecessary spending when you've financial goals to meet. If you stay on the side of caution, you'll make better financial decisions and not run into debt and financial stress. That's the best way to go about it.

Secondly, Shun comparison. Have you heard of the word Imposter syndrome?. This is a feeling of self doubt and personal incompetence which often affects those who are drawn to shiny items. Comparison is one of the primary reasons for imposter syndrome. When you compare your accomplishments or success with that of others, you might feel like a failure. Humans have a tendency to compare themselves to others. Stop obsessing over what other people are doing. The view that some people are ahead of you might make you feel trapped and encourage you to pursue shiny and interesting endeavors. Which might end up being a waste of time and effort to watch what these individuals are doing. To stop comparing you must trust and believe in yourself, as doing this will boost your self-confidence resulting in you sticking to your course and setting higher and definite goals.

There will always be those who are better off than you, therefore there is no use in comparing yourself to them. There will also be some who have it worse. It is therefore useless to compare. You'll feel resentful, unhappy, and dissatisfied if you continuously compare yourself to those who are better than you. That is not the way to live.

Also, you won't be inspired to improve yourself if you seldom measure yourself against people who have it worse off as this will give the belief that you are doing fine, and complacency might result from this. Striving for your personal growth and milestones should thus be your motto. Your greatest adversary is you. Always strive to outperform your previous achievements. You will continue to succeed if your objective is to outperform your prior wins. Never compare.

LAW #7 END FINANCIAL PRESSURE FROM PEERS/FAMILY

I will start this chapter by borrowing an American actor Will Smith popular phrase "Too many people buy things they don't need to impress people they don't like"

Simply managing one's own finances might be challenging. Things can get much more challenging when friends and families are involved. People at some point may find it difficult to strike a balance between doing what their family and societal trends deem to be right and managing their finances responsibly. The major drawback of being forced to spend excessive amounts of money is that you may find yourself falling far short of your objectives or, worse yet, incurring significant debt. In the words of Morgan Housel, a partner at collaborative fund, "Spending money to show people how much money you have is the fastest way to have less money." Now, let's look at practical ways to eliminate financial peer pressure.

- Open up: If you experience pressure, keep in mind that your friends don't want you to feel bad. Financial peer pressure most of the time happens when this person/persons want to carry you along. They truly want you to join them for movies or a trip to Florida. You must keep in mind that they probably have different financial obligations. Perhaps they don't have any school loans to worry about or aren't investing for a home right now. Maybe they just don't think you should put money down for a rainy day. They might have received a significant raise at work, but they aren't considering the fact that others might not be in the same financial situation as them. In other words, strive to be honest rather than furious. Start by discussing money issues honestly with those who are close to you. Share your financial goals and challenges. Eliminate pretense or a false sense of belonging since these things could make your friends or family feel a bit caught off guard when next you decide to skip a vacation or a social event. They will most likely serve as your largest source of support if you strive to include them in your financial plans.

- Cut off Bad Financial instigators: You should identify the person who exerts the greatest peer pressure on you. When attempting to manage your finances wisely, financial enhancers are the very last thing you need. These are the ones that amp up peer pressure and tell you convincing things to increase your spending. You shouldn't associate with people who have poor financial habits if you want encouragement to stay within your budget. Although friends can be convincing, and some may try to attach their relationship with you to your capacity to spend money with them, in the end you will be the one to face the consequences of excessive spending. Good companions will be aware of your limitations. Strive to adhere to your spending plan. The only friends worth spending time with are those that respect you and your financial objectives.here.

LAW #8 AVOID/ELIMINATE DEBTS

This comes as the first and most significant law in this part. Always try to avoid debt. All types of debts such as personal loans, credit card debt, school loan debt, etc. These debts should not be taken on. Get rid of them. Quite understandable if you have to get a business start up or expansion loan. Just be sure you can pay the bills on time each month. Remember that having some debt won't necessarily be a negative thing and you are not alone on this. For example, a mortgage can help you realize your goal of home ownership and might even help you accumulate wealth if your house grows in value.

Mortgages, credit cards, personal loans, bills, and school loans are just a few of the debts that are drowning Americans. Also, Your health may be stressed out if you have a lot of debt. The stress of not knowing how to pay the bills and the battle to put money aside for the future tends to cause financial stress, and financial stress might make it harder to keep a budget or save money. Getting out of debt may improve both your physical and emotional health. Financial confidence, morale, and possibilities to invest for the future may all increase when more money is available due to debt relief. With the correct plan, you may begin working toward debt relief while securing your money against unexpected difficulties. Take the following actionable steps into account when planning to manage your debt:

Short term strategies for managing debt: Debt reduction strategies are now essential for good money management. One thing to note is that debts should not only be fully repaid and interest should be kept to a minimum, but that it should also be done promptly. Once you have taken account of all the debts you owe and are ready to follow a repayment strategy. You may want to look at these two short term methods of debt repayment.

1. Avalanche method: Debt avalanche can be a suitable fit if you're looking for a strategy that reduces your interest costs. A common method for speeding up debt payback is debt avalanche. As the name

suggests, it's a method to assist you in paying off your debt more quickly. This method focuses on paying off your debt with the highest interest rate first before moving on to the debt with the next highest interest rate (also known as the APR). This does not imply that you overlook all of your other debts. Instead, you should pay the minimum amount due on each debt each month while also making additional payments on the one with the highest interest rate. When interest rates on loans or credit card balances are excessive, it may seem as though you would never be debt-free. This is due to the fact that the interest is accruing so quickly that if you only make the minimum payment, you might end up repaying the loan's interest alone each month. This strategy goal is to cut down on the overall interest you pay and, as a result, the overall cost of paying off your debt. You will ultimately pay less on your overall debt by paying off the debt with the highest interest rate first. The debt avalanche approach is a popular option since it is simple to implement and doesn't call for professional financial guidance. The six stages listed below can be used as a starting point.

- Determine your monthly disposable income: How much money do you have left once you've covered your vital costs, such as food, rent, utilities, etc?. Your disposable income is what you can spend to pay off debt.

- Make a note of every loan you have, no matter how minor. After making all of your notes, group them according to their interest rates. The debt with the highest interest rate should be paid off using your available cash.
- Check your minimum monthly payments: There are due dates and ongoing costs associated with your loans. Examine these specifics, then include them in your list of debts.
- Every month, carry out the aforementioned procedure until the debt with the highest interest rate is completely paid. The money you used to pay can then be applied as a new payment toward the loan with the second-highest interest rate.
- Keep doing this until your second loan is fully paid off. This process will be repeated until all of your loans have been paid off, including the one with the lowest interest rate.

You must determine your financial situation and how much you can allocate to debt repayment. The ideal budgeting strategy is to keep track of your monthly income and spending so you can know exactly how much money is coming in and going out. Finding out your overall income and spending may also be done by accessing the transactional history in your bank or credit card accounts. Knowing your monthly income and expenses can help you determine how much would be applicable to debt repayment after you must have paid the required bills and expenses. This sum will be used to pay the minimum amount owed on all debts, with any remaining funds going toward the debt with the highest interest rate.

Another debt repayment approach, the debt snowball method, is sometimes contrasted with the debt avalanche method. Both of these strategies work toward eliminating your debt, but they do it in different ways. The goal of a debt avalanche is to pay off the debts with the highest interest rates first. "On the other hand, the debt snowball strategy makes you focus on the debt with the smallest balance first." The snowball strategy is paying the minimum amount owed on all of your bills while also applying any extra funds you may have to the loan with the lowest balance. After you have paid off your smallest debt, go onto the next one with the smallest balance. Once that debt is paid off, you stop making monthly payments, which frees up cash for the next debt. Repeat the procedure until your largest debt is settled.

This approach is primarily about getting rapid wins to boost your confidence (which can be helpful if you have debt fatigue or need some motivation). You'll feel powerful as a result of the relief you get from paying off one of your debts. Both approaches have advantages and disadvantages, and one may be more appropriate in some circumstances than the other. For instance, if you desire the drive of achieving rapid wins from paying off your little debts, the debt snowball strategy can be a suitable choice. However, the debt avalanche strategy probably makes sense if you want to save money because it prioritizes paying off your high-interest debt first and lowers your overall interest costs.

Furthermore, when trying to get rid of debt. Long-term measures including debt consolidation, debt management programs, consulting services, and other outside help might be helpful for lowering debt, and that takes us to an important question.

What's debt consolidation?

Simply put, debt consolidation is the act of consolidating several debts into a single monthly payment. Rolling all of your debts into a single, streamlined payback plan saves you time and money compared to paying each creditor separately. Additionally, you attempt to lower the interest costs that have been added to your loan. As a result, you may pay off your debt more quickly since a larger portion of each payment is used to reduce the actual amount borrowed. For more in depth information on debt consolidation and other long term strategies of debt repayment visit "consolidatedcredit.org".

LAW #9 SAVE UP EMERGENCY FUNDS

An emergency savings account should be part of every financial strategy. Money set aside for unforeseen expenses is known as an emergency savings. Life's unexpected events might have an impact on your finances. You can become ill, lose your job, or need to make an expensive repair to your house or automobile. Having an emergency fund is one of the greatest methods to deal with unforeseen financial shocks. You must have 3-6 months' worth of expenses saved in case of an emergency. If you're self-employed, your income will suffer if you become sick or are admitted to the hospital since you won't be able to work (unless you have systems in place).

Eliminating certain unnecessary spending is a good way to increase your emergency funds. You probably won't be able to significantly reduce your everyday living expenditures, such as those for caregiving, clothes, housing, and transportation. However, you can reduce your discretionary spending. These are the expenses that you decide to make but may not truly need, including dining out, clubbing or night out, and impulsive purchases.

If you have an emergency fund that is well-planned and invested, you will be able to make greater long-term investments without worrying about running out of money when you need it. You'll need to have a minimum of 3 months expenses saved up in an accessible account unlike putting it in a certificate of deposit where you will be charged an early withdrawal penalty. The only good side in a certificate of deposit is that you will earn higher interest rates. Financial experts often say 3-6 months of expenses saved up will do just fine as an emergency fund. However, even that sum will only be helpful in certain crises. A 6 months expenses saved up as an emergency fund will cover you in the event of a job loss. But, If you're suffering from a serious health condition, it may not. And what if you have to stay without gainful employment because you can't find a new job in your area? Consider the kind of circumstances peculiar to you while determining if you need three, six, or more months' worth of expenses set up for emergencies.

A readily available resource, an emergency fund, can assist you in resolving monetary emergencies brought on by unforeseen events. By generating highly liquid cash to cover any emergency and lowering the need for unsecured loans, this fund helps to increase financial security. The best way to build momentum and set up an emergency fund is to start with small habitual savings by setting your beginning contribution level at an achievable amount. This will guarantee that you don't strain your cash flow and find it too simple to justify stopping your savings practice. Find an area of your life where you can cut back or live without, like your monthly coffee habit. Don't go out on a big night out or buy new designs of your favourite clothing brand. Whether it's $15 or $50, decide on an amount and make a commitment to save it on a regular basis. It could be every month, every week, or every time you are paid. The important thing is that it must become a habit rather than a continuous effort.

LAW #10 CONTRIBUTE TO SEP-IRA

SEP-IRA is a sort of self-employed pension that serves as a retirement savings account for self-employed individuals. Employers through the employer's retirement plan make use of the 401(k) to provide retirement packages for their employees. However, If you work for yourself or operate a small business, you are the employer and it might become imperative to get your own retirement plan. Enter the SEP IRA, often known as the Simplified Employee Pension plan. Although SEP IRAs are accessible to businesses of all sizes, they are often more suitable for self-employed people or SMEs. Their primary edge against others is clarity and low price: Compared to other retirement plans, they require less administrative work and usually don't charge start-up or maintenance fees. However, they come with limitations that may not be suitable for bigger firms. If you work for yourself, a SEP IRA may provide the most value in terms of cost, flexibility, investment choices, and contribution limitations. A large percentage of the over 15 million self employed people in America now look at other savings options to assist in increasing the size of their retirement savings. The SEP IRA may be the retirement plan that many self-employed prefer because of its greater contribution cap and extensive flexibility. It's worth checking out.

LAW #11 HAVE A GOOD HEALTH INSURANCE

The importance of being proactive in our financial plans can't be overemphasized. Which is why planning is said to be futuristic. A well-planned life is a life that is well-lived. One of the key components of our future planning is financial planning, which should include a thoroughly thought-out strategy to cover any medical bills down the road. This is due to the fact that lifestyle diseases are becoming more prevalent and recent global situations have revealed the possibility of unexpected health issues that require funding for their treatment.

Over the past few years, healthcare expenses have increased, making the diagnosis and subsequent treatment of some conditions unaffordable. While hospital stays are expensive, the expenditures associated with returning home afterward are also increasing dramatically. Imagine having to pay the full amount out of your own pocket, and you will feel the shock of seeing your savings wiped off. In order to prevent this, we must account for health insurance when making financial plans. Insufficient insurance coverage might cause financial catastrophe if you suddenly need medical expenses. Make sure you have a reliable, comprehensive health insurance plan.

Additionally, you should set up money for dental expenses, which may be as expensive if you require a root canal treatment. Few understand the relevance of having health insurance in their financial plan as a necessary strategy to ease the stress caused by growing healthcare expenditures. A well-thought-out health insurance plan is actually an investment. To assure the continuation of your health coverage, you only need to select an adequate plan from a reputable health insurance provider and make timely monthly payments and renewals. Having a valid policy that keeps you covered even after retirement is helpful since it compensates for all medical costs, including those associated with unexpected or scheduled hospitalization. The financial security that health insurance provides makes it worthwhile to shop for it despite the sometimes-difficult procedure. You may view and compare individual health insurance policies from many carriers at once on websites like "healthcare.com". That's if your employer doesn't provide a plan or you work for yourself. These websites make it easier to compare health insurance options and assist those looking to get a fair bargain on the coverage they require.

LAW #12 HAVE AND FOLLOW A BUDGET

The only action that actually makes achieving every other financial objective possible is creating a budget. A budget is a detailed assessment of both your revenue and expenditures, including potential side jobs or investment money. Laying everything out in front of you allows you to see what you are earning and where they are going. This will let you see if you're currently on track to reach your goals. Examining how much money comes in and being spent regularly is the first stage in developing a budget for any length of time. The more data you can compile, the better.

First and foremost, budgeting enables you to maintain your attention on your short-term and long-term objectives. Budgeting is important for many reasons, but it's especially important during uncertain times. An effective budget may help you manage your resources, actively expand them, and ensure stability and safety for you, your family, and your future, much like regular goal-setting. Creating and maintaining a budget can also aid in emergency planning. The world can be a dangerous place, as we have seen with recent events, so having a backup plan may provide you and your family peace of mind.

Start with a yearly budget, To create an annual budget, add together all the data you initially acquired and calculate the totals over a 12-month period. This calls for multiplying your monthly income and expenses by 12. Once you've finished that, put in any irregular payments you might have. For example, you might have an auto repair, a tax payment, or a vacation bill that always seems to creep up on you. Include these in your overall expenses as well. After all this is done, you may as well play the "what if" game after you've factored in the irregular expenses. Think about potential problems and assign them a monetary value. Things like what if your kid or pet falls ill and needs medical attention? What if you require repairs after some utilities in your house break down? How about that quarterly automobile insurance payment? These are your unforeseen expenses that you should account for while making your annual budget. Generally, You might use the well-known 50/30/20 budgeting framework to examine your current cash flow. 50% of your money on important needs. 30% on wants and 20% of your income should go toward debt reduction and savings. The 50/30/20 framework helps with setting up a good yearly budget.

Additionally, The monthly and weekly budget breakdown can be done using this formula; Monthly income and expenses multiplied by 12 (to obtain the total for the year). To get the weekly budget, all you need to do is divide the total budget of a year by 52 weeks. Subsequently, to get the monthly budget, divide the total budget of the year by 12 months. The take home here is that, you should use how often you get paid to define what type of budget suits your needs. For example, if you get paid monthly, set up a monthly budget.

Budgeting is synonymous to financial prudency. If you are serious about managing your money efficiently while living a comfortable and happy life. Then you must understand that to adequately plan for a financially secured life requires a good budgeting practice. The ability to account for every penny you make and how they are being spent will save you from unnecessary financial woes.

LAW #13 TRIM YOUR EXPENSES

Once you've figured out where your money is going, it's time to figure out how to make the most of it. The Japanese have a practice known as 'kaizen'. It means continuous improvement. You should apply kaizen to your lifestyle and constantly look for ways to reduce costs of living and become more efficient. Eliminate some variable expenses. The more costs you reduce, the more money you have left for savings and debt reduction. Many people are unwilling to reduce their spending. The concept of making adjustments that may require us to give up things we perceive to be entirely normal and vital to our life is unfathomable to many of us since we are used to living that way. However, trimming your expenses may not be as difficult as it seems. It is as simple as cooking and eating at home as opposed to eating out; You can as well go shopping with a list that you must adhere to. These and many other ways are great ways of being on the side of caution and not go overboard with your expenses.

LAW #14 IMPROVE YOUR KNOWLEDGE (Read Finance Books)

Financial literacy is the ability to manage your finances. This entails learning how to manage your finances wisely, including how to pay your bills, borrow money, save money, invest, and prepare for retirement. People who are financially savvy utilize their knowledge to make wiser judgments. Effective money management entails managing money to promote your own goals, no matter what they may be, from daily expenditure to long-term financial planning. Learn about investing in stocks, real estate, etc. by checking out a few personal finance books from your local library. Another crucial subject you should understand is retirement planning. Your ability to manage the money you earn from your business or job will improve as your financial literacy increases. The advice provided in this book is only the tip of the iceberg. There is still a lot to learn. Start now with the understanding that your investment in knowledge will pay you in the long run.

BONUS LAWS:

** Hire a certified public accountant (CPA) and discuss ways to legally reduce your taxes.

** Invest in assets like (annuities, real estate, stocks, cryptocurrency). Ensure you understand how such investment works before putting your money in it.

Conclusion

A basic grasp of personal finance and a willingness to accept personal responsibility are prerequisites for managing your own finances. That is, you don't bury yourself in debt and you make your payments on time. You acknowledge that occasionally giving up short-term needs and expectations in favor of long-term benefit is necessary. You set budgets. You cut costs. You safeguard funds. When you spend, do so responsibly. You only spend a lot of money on things that are worthwhile. You are aware of the distinction between acceptable and unacceptable debt. You also continually keep an eye on your total portfolio, which consists of your wages, savings, and investments. Additionally, you are aware of your ignorance and seek assistance when required. Financial literacy is the capacity to not allow money, or a lack thereof, come in the way of your happiness while you work hard and stay on course towards achieving a joyful retirement.

The End.

ABOUT THE AUTHOR

Justin S. Reed is a successful entrepreneur, certified educator, and author. He is known to expertly set out a pathway for people looking to build wealth and live more intentionally. After hitting rock bottom at different stages of his life, this 49 years old survivor has bounced back from several failed businesses and Financial doom.

These experiences made him strong and somehow, over the years he has amassed a lot of wealth from his online business and consultancy firm. In this book he shared little known money management and financial planning skills that helped him create and grow his wealth.

www.ingramcontent.com/pod-product-compliance
Lightning Source LLC
Chambersburg PA
CBHW050253220526

45465CB00002B/666